look and see me

Raymond Cooper

look
&
see me

A Book of Thoughts, Feelings, and Words

Order this book online at www.trafford.com
or email orders@trafford.com

Most Trafford titles are also available at major online book retailers.

Printed in the United States of America.

ISBN: 978-1-4669-9302-0 (sc)
ISBN: 978-1-4669-9303-7 (hc)
ISBN: 978-1-4669-9304-4 (e)

Library of Congress Control Number: 2013907887

Trafford rev. 01/31/2014

 www.trafford.com

North America & international
toll-free: 1 888 232 4444 (USA & Canada)
fax: 812 355 4082

For Adam

don't be afraid
   to dream
   to fall
   to live
   and to remember

It seems the time
between hello and goodbye
grows shorter with each day.
I know not at the moment
how to extend that time.
But it isn't
I tell myself
from any lack of trying.

We all seem to try
that much harder
the second time 'round,
learning from the times before.
Whether we are better people
for that, I cannot say.
I only know the times
I have felt and experienced
            were worth recording.

The following pages
are from some of those times.

                    R.C. June 1980

For the reasons
that have been,
       and those yet to come -

ONLY THOUGHTS

1.

I need to see
    to touch
    to feel
    to wonder –

to understand

2.

Hey sun
      don't go away yet.
It's only April.
surely you have
enough warmth left
to stay till June.

      It gets so cold
down here when
you're not around.
and I need you
to keep my body
warm through the
long winter months.

      Can't you stay
      just a little longer ?

My skin need not
be brown
all of the time
          but please,

leave me
one more
month
of sunshine,

          before you go.

3.

One day
in a far off world,
I promise to find you

But,
if I'm a little late –

       wait for me.

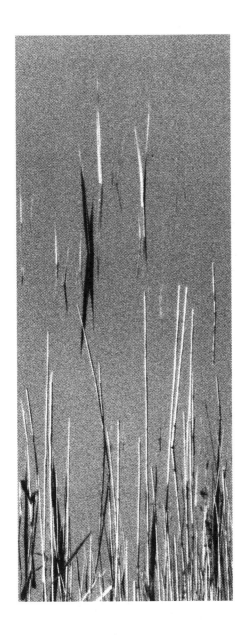

4.

What would it cost
to have your company
through the night ?

One bottle of Matues ?

I have two
        should that be your price.

5.

When
will I see you again ?

Will you write me ?
Should I wait by my telephone ?
Do you have my address ?

I miss you

6.

See the young girls
run along the beach.
See the old men
watching them.

" – dirty old men"
the young girls say.

I hope
in fifty
years time,
the young girls
are more understanding.

WINTER COMING

I need
no calendar to tell me
that winter draws nearer
with each day
    I can feel it
    in the mornings.
The trees have
all but abandoned
their leaves.
The animals too
seem to sense it,
    running desperately
looking for someone
to spend with
the cold months ahead.

I should be
out there with them –
except,

        I've walked that road
        before
and the way back
is too long and lonely.

7.

I could go back
to San Francisco
hoping to find
what I left,

I'm sure it will
    still be the same.

        But I've changed.

8.

Today
will be remembered.
because today
I climbed a high hill
and looked down
at the world

and,
     for a brief moment . . .
I understood.

9.

I find you
like the strings
of a finely tuned guitar.
As my fingers run
the length of your
body, you utter sounds
I long so much to hear.

    Lets get together tonight
and
      if I touch you
           when I touch you,
will you reward my body
as much as you do my ears ?

10.

I would
call you tonight
if I knew your number
but,
how would I begin…
let alone
maintain a conversation.

I saw you today
but you were unaware
of my sniper's eye
watching your every move.

Should I wait
for your call . . . ?

No.

My phone has been
such a silent creature.
I could ask
the phone company
to take it away,
    but I lack the courage.

11.

It's very easy for me
to write down on paper
for invisible onlookers
        my needs and wants,
mostly things
I'll never have.

It's very hard for me
to write down on paper
for your eyes only
        my feelings
                and thoughts,
things you'll never understand.

But, if you know me –
        you'll understand.

TIME

God,
I hate this
in between-time
of learning to
walk alone

all over again.

FRIDAY NIGHT

Alone
is such a familiar word lately.

What have I done to hurt you
tell me.
I'll undo it a thousand times
                    and then some.

Was it communication we lacked?
- oh God
if I knew the meaning of the word
then,
I might still have your head
next to mine at night.

So much we did
that I took for granted.
        So much I took
        so little I gave.

Ask me now what you want
and it's yours.
Ask for the world
and I would find some way of giving it
      if it were good enough.
But I know you don't want the world
        you wanted very little
        I wanted very much.
You needed caressing in the
mornings
I wanted you at night.
   -oh God, hear me.
   People change.

Let me show you.

SUNDAY MORNING

Morning –
I'm growing to hate it so much.
It just means the start of
trying to get through another
day without you,
and with each passing day
my need for you
grows more intense.

Let's go through
our box and pull out all
the bad times.
    There can't
be all that
many to pull out

    can there?

I used
to love mornings, once.
I used to wait
all night long
for them to come,
because it meant the
time we would each
become as one,
               and sometimes,
morning would last
the entire day.

But lately
            without you
mornings have become
so hard to face.

I try burying
my head in the pillow
and hope they'll go away

            -but they never do.

They have a way
of coming round

at least once every day.

SUNDAY NIGHT

I never thought
I could love
someone else so soon
after losing you.

I must have
such a thin heart

- to be able
to let someone else in
so easily.

TUESDAY

I may not
see you again.

    That's not to say
I love you any less.
I just don't think
my mind
        or my heart
is strong enough
to have you as
        just a friend.
We've explored each other
too deeply to finish
at that

Besides,
tomorrow is another day.

      Just as sure
as we've run on
Victorian beaches
and watched the last
light of day
      touch one another's head.

THURSDAY

Seeing you again
                    today
made me postpone my suicide
just that much longer.

Were you happy to see me?
              Did you miss me?
                    Can I stay?
Questions I want to ask
but,
never seem to find their
way past the strange lump
that fills my throat
when I'm near you.

Strange
I never noticed
that lump before.

I guess like
many other things
it's been there
all the time –

I just didn't notice.

SECOND FRIDAY NIGHT

My fingers tremble
as they reach to dial
your number.
My heart too, trembles,
but like an Autumn leaf
          always clinging,
while never knowing
when or where
              to fall.

I'm keeping tomorrow
free for the zoo.
I have it all worked out –
you can be feeding the
monkeys their peanuts,
while I work at getting
patiently
       inch
          by
             inch
closer to you.

I know
you won't / can't refuse.
You see,
what little hope
I have left is all
going into the next
few minutes –
        and that's
something not to be taken
very lightly.

I have been told
quite frequently
of late
by those I hold close,
that tomorrow
is another day.

    I have no reason
    to disbelieve that.

But I do know
that if today is
any example of what
tomorrow brings

I'm content to remain
a Friday man.

SECOND SUNDAY NIGHT

I feel
like writing / doing nothing.

-The day is spent

and I have nothing
or anybody
    to show for it.

PASSING THE TIME

one

I said
I could be down
your way today
        taking photographs.
Didn't you know
it was only
an excuse
        to be near you,
of hoping
to capture you
in my viewfinder.

But even
a telephoto lens
will only give
a close up
        distorted
                vision of you.

If
you see me
with my camera,
taking photographs
of your house from
a distance –

    run up to me
    and say hello.

two

the sun
felt extra warm today,
because you cared
enough to share
with me
     the only thing you have,

    -yourself.

three

Its
not very often
I'm found at home
these past weeks.
Usually,
I'm at the airport

        walking

           sitting

searching faces
for one that resembles
in the smallest way,
your face.
Watching planes
fall like rain
on their final approach.

Do you
sit at
San Francisco International
passing your time
       the same way?

four

If
you walk by me
in a vacant Sunday
car park,
or see my
tanned body
lying on a crowded
           sunny beach --

If
you pass me
in a lonely
bus depot,
or see me
sitting in
an all-night café
       looking at unfamiliar faces -

Find time
     to stop
and notice me.

 Even
a fleeting hello,
will bring a long awaited
smile to this brown
sun bleached face.

DRIVING TO ALAMEDA

I remember
a summer
many seasons ago,
when you and I
spent the afternoon
driving to the
Alameda County Fair.

I remember
winning you
a bottle of
Pinot Chardonnay
by throwing dimes
onto squares.

    Being with you
             then
my life was full.

But now,
    like the bottle of wine ....

five

I've
loved you
a long time
before arriving
at this moment.

    Today.

               Now.

And
I don't
half wish
we could do it all again.

six

I could be
content with
the warmth of
your body
     and a vintage wine.

But
the April sun
is longer lasting.

And,
to the best
of my knowledge –
     April too
has a way of
coming round
at least once
every year.

I have yet
to find a person
   as warm
      and reliable
as an April sun.

seven

If I could give
all my tomorrows
for just
one more today
            with you,
I would be happy –
                today.

But tomorrow
would be just another day.

eight

The
only present
I could think
of giving,
to justify
my feelings
in you as a friend

    was a single rose
accompanied by time.

Time to grow

to love

to feel

to experience.

Time
to be you,

as only you know how.

nine

I walked
along a beach
this morning
and spoke to
an old man.

He was
sitting there
as if waiting
for someone.

I like
to think that
    when I left –

he was wearing
a smile upon
his tired face,

even if
that someone was only me

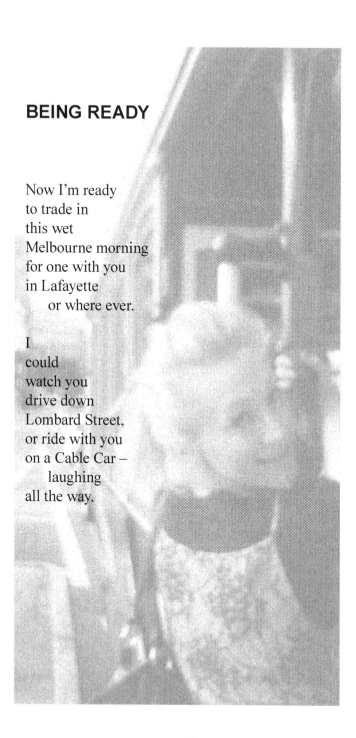

BEING READY

Now I'm ready
to trade in
this wet
Melbourne morning
for one with you
in Lafayette
        or where ever.

I
could
watch you
drive down
Lombard Street,
or ride with you
on a Cable Car –
        laughing
all the way.

Now
I'm ready
to drive along
the coast,
taking turns
at owning the
houses we pass
along the way –

first your turn

now mine.

Now
I'm ready
to do all these
things we've only
talked about on mornings
when it was too cold or wet
to do anything else except
to stay in bed and make
promises to each
other never
to part.

Now I'm ready.

Where are you ?

ten

White sneakers
and faded jeans
had been my sign
when travelling with you.

But somewhere
along the way,
and barely enough
    to hold you,
they were exchanged
for well pressed trousers
and English tweed jackets.

And now
with grey hairs
replacing the black –

       I ask
what chance
I have
       with slippers and scarf.

eleven

The dogs bark
and they don't bark -
    I don't know.
My mind is elsewhere.
I have but one hour
two if I'm lucky
before your leaving
becomes a reality.

I don't want you to go.

The closing shut
of your suitcase
is but a final sound
of your leaving.

The day is lost
        and so am I.

OPENING DOORS

Lead me down
the passages of your life.
Open doors
along the way
to show me
where you've been
and who you are –
    I need to know that
    desperately.

If the journey
is a long one
and I show signs of tiring,
prop my head
against a wall
    or better still
the warmth
of your breast.

Take my hand
if I wander
    or dally
along the way.
And if I
                should I
decide I'm
not yet ready

    keep on walking.
    But God –
don't let go

            ….please

PARK STREET

Park Street to us
was once the whole world.
It wasn't till we left
that you discovered a
new world,
waiting just outside
of ours.

But,
with new worlds
come new people.

I
wish not
to be a traveler
of alien worlds,
    but of time.

My suitcase
stands packed
    filled full
with white sneakers
and tweed jackets,
ready
at a minutes notice
to be given that ticket –

        a ticket to
        a time when

Park Street to us
was once the whole world.

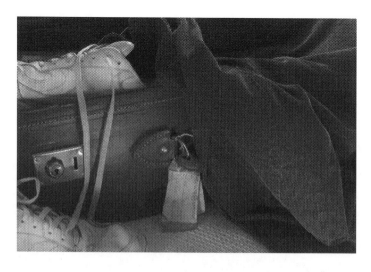

twelve

Our marriage plans
are all but finished.
These past days
have been devoted
    to just that.
The church has been chosen.
The guest list is written.

How does this tie look?
    Or this one here?
I can buy another
if brown or green
is not to your liking.

I know
so little
about your
likes and dislikes
    Not to worry.
    Not to worry.

In time
I'll set out
with compass and map,
taking care not
to tire on the way.
But
at the same time
taking care not
to go too far
     too soon.

And
     if I
               should I
trek deep enough
to reach your thoughts
     I'll leave
something of myself
a sign to those
who come later,
that someone
had been here
before them.

I'll set out also
to find new lands
     One in which
to spend a honeymoon
     One in which
to spend a life.

I haven't
found them yet,
but I keep on looking –

        as I keep
        a lookout, still
                for you….

FROM YOU

I made it
through Monday
without you –
but that's
not to say
thoughts
of you
weren't
at the back
of my mind,
creeping forwards
    unawares.

Now
its night –
distant coughing,
              traffic,
                        music,
reaches
but does not penetrate.

Here
there is
only a flickering flame –
slowly
disappearing
over the rim
of the candle.

     -last night
it cast shadows
of love on the wall.

But that
was last night –

now you're gone

-Shelly

JUNE 3

How I've come this
far and still go
on without you
is questionable.
Surely at the time
I knew I
wouldn't / couldn't
make half the distance.

I stand still a minute
maybe two,
and ask –

What now ?
Where now ?
Who now ?

I don't half
mind admitting
(even to myself)
that I'm afraid
of the July Sundays
ahead – weary from
the ones behind.

But,
I've promised
myself a November
(should I make it that far)

A November
filled full with
hills of hope

    -sitting there
waiting to be climbed.

Should I not
survive this
final journey,
this last attempt
to find that elusive
something
        someone
                somewhere

-then I will know it
 was God's own will.

I'm ready once more,

        ....are you ?

and now

one.

here I am again

       or there,

one or the other is true...

two.

Run to my house
and call
my name aloud.
I live
but one block further
and down a bit.

Run to my house
with pockets of
friendship.

Run to my door
and call my name.

Should I not answer
when two dozen shouts
or half
of that
has passed
than
know that I am gone.

But also know
that I waited
                    still for you ….

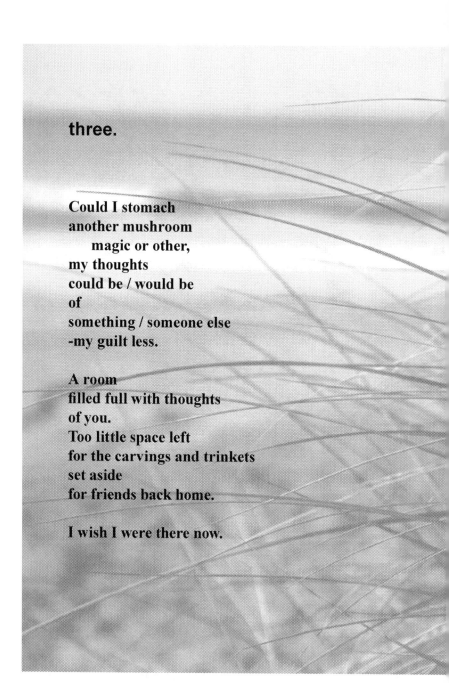

three.

Could I stomach
another mushroom
    magic or other,
my thoughts
could be / would be
of
something / someone else
-my guilt less.

A room
filled full with thoughts
of you.
Too little space left
for the carvings and trinkets
set aside
for friends back home.

I wish I were there now.

Two weeks set aside

to forget
four years and you.

four.

Your smiles
invite me into your life.
Your looks
say hi
across an empty room.

And though
you're only
    a bedroom away
the doors between
are worlds apart.

But that's ok,
I have been known
to travel worlds
    that were not mine
to travel

-given the chance.

five.

Sing me a song
write me a poem
play me a tune
I don't yet know.

Speak to me slowly
of fire
    and Fridays
of Summers wind
    and Winters snow.

Please,
sing me a song
but use few words
my span of attention
is five minutes

      no more.

I'll meet the mailman.

You promised to write
from Auckland, Lafayette,
    or where ever.

Not to worry.

With new faces
and fresh smiles
that jump out
and rape me
    from nowhere,
my concentration
is but two lines
            no more.

But should the smiles
disappear
-and I know
they will

then
I'll meet
the mailman

once again.

six.

Your memory
still lingers.

But
like the fragrance
    you left behind

grows more faint
with each day...

seven.

I know
I'm not your white knight
    in shining armour.

I may not
have even made it
onto your list
of favorite heroes.

But,
given the time
    and half a chance,
I challenge anyone

    -in armour or cape

who dares to think
he can love you

        more than me.

eight.

Can I be
of any help
with your suitcase
    or your trunk ?

Can I stack
your firewood
    against the door ?

If your heads too heavy
filled full
with thoughts and concern,
let it lean
against this already
    crooked arm.

Have you packages
of love
that need untying
    and tying up ?

Let me first
unfold your smile
and bend it
to my own

....that's a beginning.

nine.

I wish
I had a camera
to photograph the yellow tulips.
Seven of them
still stay alive
     staring at the ceiling
as if the sun shone there.

That kind of optimism
frightens me of late.
Even here in this room
filled full
     with things I hold close.

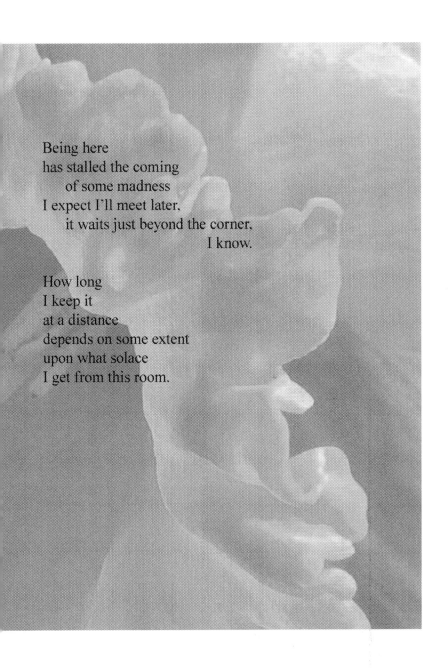

Being here
has stalled the coming
     of some madness
I expect I'll meet later,
     it waits just beyond the corner,
                              I know.

How long
I keep it
at a distance
depends on some extent
upon what solace
I get from this room.

ten.

Am I to believe
that what and who
delivered me to this day
here
and now
was for a reason ?

Where did I come from ?
        Why me ?

Was this my mothers grand plan
to put me here
        today ?
Was this the reason
she staggered and stumbled
with me in her arms ?

Why she fed me her milk
of human kindness
so that one day
I could form a fist
just big enough
to sometimes
get my own way.

Was her bent back
and tired eyes
worth what I see in the mirror ?

What did I expect to find ?

More than what my son
sees
when I walk into the room ?

I would
wish for them
something
someone better.

Perhaps tomorrow
will show
a more handsome
and stronger reflection.

That's a thought
not to be taken lightly.